Snail in the Woods

HARPER & ROW, PUBLISHERS
NEW YORK

Cambridge London
Hagerstown Mexico City
Philadelphia Sao Paolo
San Francisco Sydney

1817

Weekly Reader Books presents

Snail in the Woods
by Joanne Ryder

with the assistance of Harold S. Feinberg

pictures by Jo Polseno

A Nature I CAN READ Book

Acknowledgment

*I would like to thank The New York Shell Club
and especially Bruce Einsohn for
their help in locating living snails for observation.*

This book is a presentation of Weekly Reader Books.
Weekly Reader Books offers book clubs for children from
preschool through junior high school.

For further information write to:
Weekly Reader Books
1250 Fairwood Ave.
Columbus, Ohio 43216

SNAIL IN THE WOODS
Text copyright © 1979 by Joanne Ryder
Illustrations copyright © 1979 by Jo Polseno

Library of Congress Cataloging in Publication Data
Ryder, Joanne.
  Snail in the woods.

  (A Nature I can read book)
  SUMMARY: A snail's life from the time it is hatched
to the time it lays its own eggs.
  1. Mesodon thyroidus—Juvenile literature.
2. Snails—Juvenile literature. [1. Snails]
I. Feinberg, Harold S. II. Polseno, Jo. III. Title.
QL430.5.P6R93 1979   594'.38   78-22157
ISBN 0-06-025168-9
ISBN 0-06-025169-7 lib. bdg.

Many snails must live underwater. They live hidden lives in oceans and ponds, and when they die only their empty shells are washed ashore.

But some snails are air-breathing animals and live on land.

Most land snails are the same sex. There are no male and female snails. When snails mate, each one can fertilize the eggs in the other snail's body. All snails can lay eggs. Since so many animals eat land snails, it is important that all the snails that survive can lay eggs and produce more snails.

The snail in this book belongs to the species *Mesodon thyroidus*. It has a curled brown shell which is tilted to one side. When you see the snail in the woods or in this book, you can see the curled whorls clearly from some viewpoints but not all. As the snail grows, the shell grows too. When the snail is full-grown, a white edge or lip appears on the shell. So the snail is known as the common white-lipped snail.

**For Darlene Abdale,
biologist, teacher, and good friend**

Near a river

large oak trees grow.

It is late spring,

and the trees are full

of new green leaves.

Old dead leaves

cover the ground.

Under the dead leaves,

it is cool and dark.

Hidden there

is a curled, brown shell

one inch long.

After sunset,

the brown shell moves.

A small head

and long, thin body

appear under the shell.

It is a common white-lipped snail.

The snail crawls

to a log under an oak.

It makes a hole

in the soft, wet earth.

The snail lays 40 eggs

in the hole.

It covers the hole

and crawls away.

Later, a shrew

digs under the log.

She uncovers some of the eggs

and eats them

until an owl swoops near

and scares her.

A few eggs

are still hidden.

Three weeks later,

the first snail

gnaws a hole

in its eggshell

and crawls out.

For its first meal,

the snail eats

its own eggshell.

The snail's tiny body

is soft and boneless.

On its back,

the snail has

a pale, curled shell.

It is part of the snail.

During the hot day,

the tiny snail rests

tucked inside its shell.

Later rain falls.

The late afternoon

is cool and cloudy,

and the snail crawls out.

It is looking for food.

It glides across a leaf

on its long, flat foot.

Near the front of the foot,

there is a tiny pore

in the snail's body.

From this tiny pore

seeps a wet path

of sticky mucus.

The snail glides easily

on this wet path

and leaves a shiny trail behind.

Yet the snail crawls slowly.

It takes the snail

at least a minute

to crawl over a two-inch leaf.

The snail has

two pairs of feelers on its head.

At the tip

of each of the two long feelers

is a black dot.

These are the snail's eyes.

The snail stretches

one of its long feelers

even longer.

It can see the grayness ahead.

The snail twists

its other feeler

under the leaf.

Now it sees

the darkness there, too.

18

Under the leaf

a millipede is hiding.

It moves and touches

the snail's feeler.

Quickly, the snail

pulls its feeler back.

19

The tiny eye glides down

the center of the feeler

until it is hidden

inside the snail's head.

The snail waits

and then stretches its feeler.

The black eye glides

up to the tip again.

Feeling its way,

the snail crawls to another leaf.

Thin threads of fungus

are growing there.

The snail scrapes off

bits of fungus to eat.

All summer long,

whenever it is

cool and damp and dark,

the snail eats.

Sometimes it climbs up

the prickly nettles

and eats their leaves.

The snail's soft body is growing,

and so is its hard shell.

From the hills,

the river carries

bits of limestone to the woods.

There is lime in the soil

and in the plants

the snail eats.

The snail's body needs lime

to make its shell grow

larger and darker and thicker.

In October,

the oak leaves turn brown

and fall to the ground.

The days are colder.

Many woodland birds

fly south.

The snail hides under a stone.

It pulls its body

inside its shell,

and it makes a hard seal

over the opening.

26

Its heartbeat slows

and the snail rests.

In the ground,

other animals and insects

are sleeping, too.

But some animals stay awake.

All winter long, the shrews dig

under stones and logs

to find sleeping snails.

The shrews store the snails

in hiding places.

And when they are hungry,

they come and eat the snails.

The shrews find many snails

in the woods,

but not the small snail.

In the spring,

the first warm rain

falls in the woods.

It drips on the ground

and seeps under the stone

where the small snail is resting.

The snail wakes up.

It breaks open

the seal to its shell

and eats it.

Soon other snails

are crawling in the leaves.

They absorb the rain

through their skins.

They store some of the water

inside their shells.

In the dark,

the snails hunt for food.

But other animals

are hunting, too.

Many woodland animals eat snails.

Birds and moles eat snails.

Tiny glowworms eat them.

Even some kinds of snails

eat other snails.

From under the stone,

the small snail crawls out

and begins eating.

A white-footed mouse

leaps so quickly,

the snail does not

see or sense the danger.

The mouse bites

the snail's long feeler.

The snail quickly

hides inside its shell.

But the mouse drags

the shell away.

Suddenly, something

grabs the mouse.

An owl carries the mouse

up to her nest.

Squealing, the mouse

drops the small snail.

It falls against a stone

and chips its shell.

The snail is hurt,

but in time

it will be well again.

The snail can grow

a new feeler.

Lime from its body will fill

the crack in the shell.

For several weeks,

it does not rain.

Other animals

move nearer the river.

The snail has no more water

stored inside its shell.

Without water,

the snail cannot make

its sticky path.

Its soft body will dry up.

So the snail rests.

It seals itself inside its shell.

It does not come out again

until it rains.

By September,

the snail's shell

is one inch long.

There are five whorls in the shell,

and around the opening

there is a new white lip.

The snail is full-grown now.

It is ready to mate.

One fall evening,

the snail touches

something soft,

something alive.

It is another snail.

The snail has a white lip

on its shell, too.

The snails stroke each other

with their long feelers.

And they mate.

Shortly after mating,

the white-lipped snail

finds a place to rest.

During the long winter,

the shrews eat the snail's mate,

but they do not find the snail.

When the days get warmer,

the snail wakes again.

In the warm spring,

it rains for days and days.

The river floods the woods.

Some snails climb trees.

They cling to the tree trunks

and move higher as the waters rise.

Floating logs and branches

carry snails and insects away.

The white-lipped snail

is on the old log.

Snakes and turtles swim past

as the log floats away.

Up in the trees,

white-footed mice hide.

Finally, the floodwaters go down.

But the flood

has changed the woods.

Dead leaves were washed away,

and many of the old landmarks

are gone.

So are some of the animals.

Worms and glowworms drowned.

Several shrews drowned, too.

The snails that are left

crawl to the ground

and find new places to hide.

Half a mile away

the old log rests

near a large tree.

The snail still clings

to the log.

There are oak trees

and nettles here.

This new place

will be the snail's home.

One night,

the snail lays

30 eggs under the log.

Soon there will be

more snails

in this part of the woods.

PARTS OF THE SNAIL

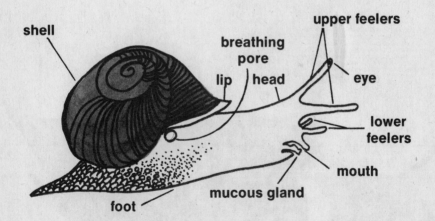

shell

breathing pore

upper feelers

lip   head

eye

lower feelers

mouth

mucous gland

foot